THIS JOURNAL &
BOOK OF CHEERS

BELONGS TO:

_____

_____

_____

CHEER NAME	PAGE

CHEER NAME	PAGE

3

CHEER NAME:_____

_____
_____
_____
_____
_____
_____
_____
_____
_____
_____
_____
_____
_____
_____
_____
_____

TEAM
SPIRIT

CHEER NAME:_____

_____
_____
_____
_____
_____

CHEER NAME:_____

_____
_____
_____
_____
_____

5

CHEER NAME:_____

BIG-G
LITTLE-O
GO - GO!

6

CHEER NAME:_____

_____
_____
_____
_____
_____
_____
_____
_____
_____
_____
_____
_____
_____
_____
_____
_____
_____
_____
_____
_____

CHEER NAME:_____

V
I
C
T
O
R
Y

8

CHEER NAME:_____

_____
_____
_____
_____
_____
_____
_____
_____

9

CHEER NAME:_____

_____
_____
_____
_____
_____
_____
_____
_____
_____
_____

READY?
OK!

CHEER NAME:_____

11

CHEER NAME:_____

_____
_____
_____
_____
_____
_____
_____
_____
_____
_____
_____

12

GO TEAM!!

CHEER NAME:_____

_____
_____
_____
_____
_____
_____
_____
_____
_____
_____

13

CHEER NAME:_____

_____
_____
_____
_____
_____
_____
_____
_____
_____
_____
_____
_____
_____
_____
_____
_____
_____
_____

TEAM
SPIRIT

14

CHEER NAME:_____

_____
_____
_____
_____
_____

CHEER NAME:_____

_____
_____
_____
_____
_____

CHEER NAME:_____

BIG-G,
LITTLE-O
GO - GO!

16

CHEER NAME:_____

CHEER NAME:_____

V
I
C
T
O
R
Y

18

CHEER NAME:_____

CHEER NAME:_____

_____
_____
_____
_____
_____
_____
_____
_____
_____
_____
_____

READY?
OK!

CHEER NAME:_____

_____
_____
_____
_____
_____
_____
_____
_____

CHEER NAME:_____

_____
_____
_____
_____
_____
_____
_____

21

CHEER NAME:_____

GO TEAM!!

CHEER NAME:_____

_____

_____

_____

_____

_____

_____

_____

_____

_____

_____

CHEER NAME:_____

_____
_____
_____
_____
_____
_____
_____
_____
_____
_____
_____
_____
_____
_____
_____
_____

TEAM
SPIRIT

CHEER NAME:_____

_____
_____
_____
_____
_____

CHEER NAME:_____

_____
_____
_____
_____
_____

25

CHEER NAME:_____

BIG-G,
LITTLE-O
GO - GO!

26

CHEER NAME:_____

CHEER NAME:_____

V
I
C
T
O
R
Y

28

CHEER NAME:_____

CHEER NAME:_____

READY?
OK!

30

CHEER NAME:_____

CHEER NAME:_____

31

CHEER NAME:_____

GO TEAM!!

CHEER NAME:_____

_____

_____

_____

_____

_____

_____

_____

_____

_____

_____

CHEER NAME:_____

_____
_____
_____
_____
_____
_____
_____
_____
_____
_____
_____
_____
_____
_____
_____
_____
_____

TEAM SPIRIT

CHEER NAME:_____

_____
_____
_____
_____
_____

CHEER NAME:_____

_____
_____
_____
_____
_____

CHEER NAME:_____

BIG-G,
LITTLE-O,
GO - GO!

36

CHEER NAME:_____

CHEER NAME:_____

VICTORY

CHEER NAME:_____

CHEER NAME:_____

_____
_____
_____
_____
_____
_____
_____
_____
_____
_____

READY?
OK!

40

CHEER NAME:_____

CHEER NAME:_____

41

CHEER NAME:_____

42

GO TEAM!!

CHEER NAME:_____

_____
_____
_____
_____
_____
_____
_____
_____
_____
_____

CHEER NAME:_____

_____
_____
_____
_____
_____
_____
_____
_____
_____
_____
_____
_____
_____
_____
_____
_____
_____

TEAM
SPIRIT

CHEER NAME:_____

_____
_____
_____
_____
_____

CHEER NAME:_____

_____
_____
_____
_____
_____

45

CHEER NAME:_____

BIG-G
LITTLE-O
GO - GO!

46

CHEER NAME:_____

CHEER NAME:_____

VICTORY

49

MY "LIFE IS AWESOME" JOURNAL

USE THE PROMPTS AT THE TOP OF EACH
PAGE FOR IDEAS TO WRITE ABOUT

ALWAYS REMEMBER:
YOU ARE A BEAUTIFUL,
ONE-OF-A-KIND,
AWESOME PERSON.

I LOVE BEING A CHEERLEADER BECAUSE...

DESCRIBE A PERFECT DAY

53

MY BEST FRIEND IS MY BEST FRIEND BECAUSE

NAME 3 THINGS THAT MAKE YOU FEEL HAPPY

WHO IS THE FUNNIEST PERSON YOU KNOW? WHY?

I KNOW MY PARENTS LOVE ME BECAUSE

WHAT IS YOUR DREAM PET?

IF SOMEONE GAVE YOU $1 MILLION DOLLARS TODAY, WHAT WOULD YOU DO WITH IT?

MAKE A LIST OF 10 THINGS YOU ARE GOOD AT

MY EARLIEST MEMORY IS

WHAT DO YOU WANT TO BE WHEN YOU GROW UP?   WHY?

WHAT IS THE MOST BEAUTIFUL THING YOU HAVE EVER SEEN?

65

MY FAVORITE FOODS/MEALS ARE...

67

NAME 3 GOALS YOU HAVE SET FOR YOURSELF

LIST 3 THINGS YOU ADMIRE ABOUT YOUR PARENTS

71

I AM GRATEFUL FOR _____ (FAMILY MEMBER) BECAUSE...

_____

WHAT IS THE BRAVEST THING YOU HAVE EVER DONE?

LAST NIGHT I HAD THE CRAZIEST DREAM...

IF YOU COULD GO ANYWHERE IN THE WORLD WHERE WOULD YOU GO?

MAKE A LIST OF YOUR FAVORITE PET NAMES
(YOU CAN REFER TO IT LATER WHEN YOU GET THAT DREAM PET!)

I AM GRATEFUL FOR _____ (TEACHER)
BECAUSE...

IF YOU HAD 3 WISHES, WHAT WOULD THEY BE?

WHAT ARE 3 QUALITIES YOU LOVE ABOUT YOURSELF?

WHAT DO YOU DO WHEN YOU SEE A CLASSMATE STRUGGLING WITH SOMETHING?

I AM GRATEFUL FOR _____ (FRIEND)
BECAUSE...

WHO IS THE PERSON YOU TRUST THE MOST? WHY?

89

91

WHAT IS YOUR FAVORITE HOBBY OR CRAFT?

WRITE ABOUT A PERSON YOU ADMIRE

93

WHAT ARE YOUR FAVORITE THINGS TO DO ON A SUMMER DAY?

WRITE ABOUT A TIME YOU HELPED ANOTHER PERSON. HOW DID IT MAKE YOU FEEL?

I AM GRATEFUL FOR_____(SOMETHING IN NATURE)
BECAUSE...

97

IF YOUR PET COULD TALK
HOW WOULD THEY DESCRIBE THEIR DAY?

IF SOMEONE WERE TRAVELING TO YOUR TOWN, WHAT WOULD YOU SUGGEST THEY DO OR SEE?

I LOVE MY AWESOME LIFE BECAUSE..

Made in the USA
Columbia, SC
01 April 2021